DIVINE teaTime

INSPIRATION CARDS

Rituals and blends to soothe your soul

TRACY LOUGHLIN

Contents

HERB

1. Borage flowers and lemon tea
2. Chamomile, catnip and citrus tea
3. Lavender and mint tea
4. Lemon balm sun tea
5. Lemongrass tea
6. Olive leaf tea
7. Oregano tea
8. Pine needle tea
9. Sage and lemon tea
10. Thyme, tarragon and verbena tea

FLOWER

11. Cherry blossom (sakura) tea
12. Dandelion tea
13. Echinacea tea
14. Elderflower tea
15. Hibiscus and rose sun tea
16. Hibiscus tea
17. Honeysuckle tea
18. Lavender and chamomile tea
19. Red clover tea
20. Rose hip and lemon tea

FRUIT

21. Blueberry, lemon and rosemary tea
22. Berry fruit tea
23. Lemon, lime, mint and cucumber tea
24. Lychee and mint tea
25. Peach, ginger and green tea
26. Pineapple, lime and coconut tea
27. Raspberry, blueberry and cinnamon tea
28. Strawberry, basil and mint tea
29. Thyme and blood orange tea
30. Watermelon, orange and coriander tea

SPICE

31. Apple and ginger tea
32. Cardamom, rose and borage tea
33. Cardamom tea
34. Clove tea
35. Mango, raspberry and ginger tea
36. Pepper tea
37. Rhubarb spiced tea
38. Star anise, fennel and cinnamon tea
39. Tamarind, hibiscus and ginger tea
40. Turmeric and black pepper tea

Introduction

Welcome to *Divine Tea Time Inspiration Cards*, a collection of illustrated tea recipes inspired by herbs and flowers you can grow, as well as spices you may have in your pantry, and fruit from the local fruit and vegetable shop or supermarket.

Tea making is quite simple, you only need two ingredients to start, just pick a handful of mint from the garden, wash and place it in a glass, add boiled water, let it brew for a few minutes and you have a refreshing drink.

Most of the recipes in the *Divine Tea Time Inspiration Cards* set use 1 litre/quart water measure but the iced teas and the sun teas use a standard size jug as the measure to fill.

My collection is just the start in an ongoing journey of tea making. Inspired by a couple of old herb and spice books I use as a reference for drawings, I started doing some research then making simple tea experiments using what I had in my garden and spice cupboard. I created the illustrations and recipes over the spring and summer seasons and have used fresh herbs and flowers in my recipes. You can also buy dried flowers, spices and herbs from specialty tea shops and spice shops or online.

Mixing your own recipes of flowers, spices and herbs can become a calming time during the day when you focus on preparing a special tea, gathering ingredients, letting the water boil and then enjoying what you created. It could be a cool, refreshing summer tea or a medicinal warming drink when you are feeling low and needing a pick-me-up. You don't need a lot of space for a few pots – a balcony or a windowsill is enough to grow some of your favourite herbs to use fresh, or cut and dry them for another time.

This deck can be used as an inspirational set of tea recipes to enjoy, and hopefully it will start many people experimenting with what's in their garden and fridge and coming up with new mixes and flavours.

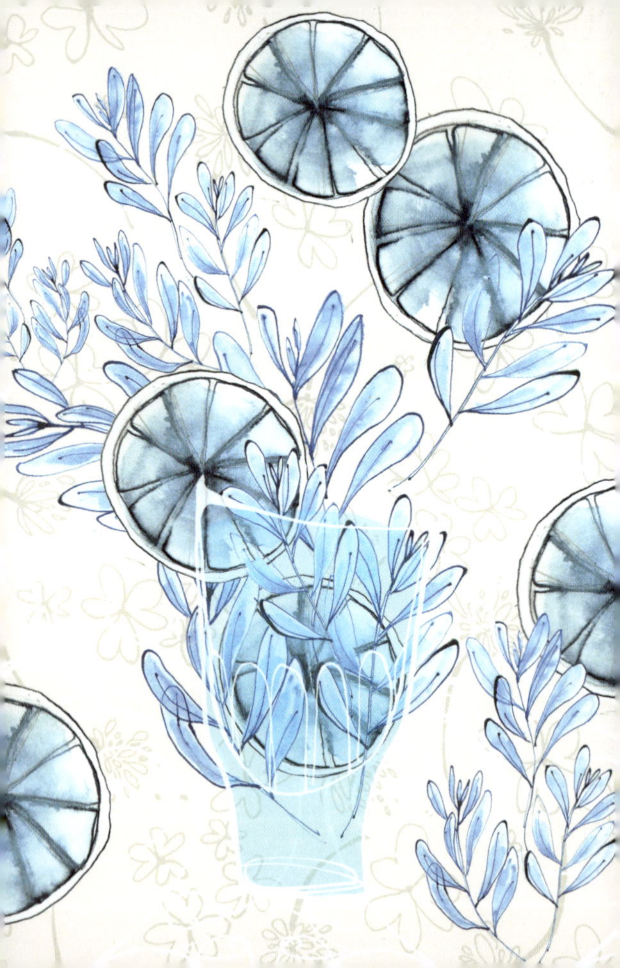

Recipe selections

I've broken up my *Divine Tea Time Inspiration Cards* set into 4 types of ingredients – fruit, flower, herb and spice. I hope these recipes are a springboard for your own experiments. Some of the recipes are not true tea – I have included some fruit and herb infusions as the weather where I live is hot and that's what was needed at the time. So get inventive and have a play.

As an added note to each recipe, I have finished with a key word that describes one of the benefits each tea will bring from drinking it. There are many benefits teas have on the body but don't overdo it. A litre/quart of water, 4 cups per day of tea is all you need. It may only take one to send you to your special tea place.

HERB

Inspired by my garden and my rosemary, oregano, thyme and mint cuttings, I've tried to keep the recipes simple and easy so you can go out with your scissors, cut a sprig or two and just add water.

These ingredients can also be used dried and are available in specialist tea shops, herb and spice shops or online. Make sure your ingredients have not been sprayed with pesticides. Do some research into what herbs you like and find out the best ways to use them in tea making.

Also a special note for the pine needle tea – you should not drink this if you are pregnant. Avoid yew or cypress which can be mistaken for pine as well. Norfolk Island Pine should not be used. Pine needle tea can be bought in tea shops or online if you don't have access to the correct pine species.

If catnip is not available it may be substituted with chamomile flowers, Valerian root or Tatarian honeysuckle flowers.

FLOWER

Picking flowers from the garden or doing some foraging can be most satisfying when you are rewarded with a wonderful flower tea to look at and drink. I have included a couple of petals here you may need to purchase instead of growing your own.

The cherry blossom flowers are specialty items but so beautiful I had to include them. You may be able to purchase them from Asian supermarkets - if not try a specialty tea shop or online is also an option. Dried petals and mixes are available from tea and spice shops. You can also purchase edible flowers from some specialty fruit and vegetable shops.

FRUIT

Some of the fruit recipes are just infusion and perhaps should not be called tea, but as they are generally what is called for on hot summer days, they take the place of a traditional tea a lot of the time. Therefore I have included some experiments that will refresh you. These are a bit more complex with 3 and 4 ingredients, but they are delicious and make a great jug for the table or an afternoon cool down. You can also experiment with adding a litre/quart extra of tea made from your favourite black tea blend to any of the infusions or even a litre/quart of coconut water to add a real fresh blast to a chilled fusion mix.

You can use frozen fruits in most of the recipes, but I'm not sure about frozen watermelon. I have not tried that as I used what was in season at my local fruit shops and the lychee tea uses tinned fruit.

SPICE

I started using simple single spices from my cupboard for these recipes. I was hesitant at first, using only pepper, cardamom and clove but I was surprised at how cleansing they felt. There are a couple of recipes that involve more than just adding to hot water, but these mixes are well worth the time it takes.

Once again, all spices can be found in your local supermarket. I've combined a couple of herbs and flowers that can be purchased at specialist tea or spice shops. The spice and fruit mixes here are worth your while testing out - apple and ginger make a lovely warm winter drink and the rhubarb is great in summer as a cool iced tea, so get cooking.

I hope you find the *Divine Tea Time Inspiration Cards* set a pleasure to look at and an inspiration for you to start experimenting with flowers, fruits, herbs and spices to come up with your own signature recipes. Don't forget to research ingredients and make sure they are suitable for tea making. You can't just pull out any weed or pluck any berry from a bush and brew it up. Some herbs and flowers are not suitable for tea making or cooking with, so dive into a few books and find out about your ingredients if you want to experiment with anything not commonly used in tea making.

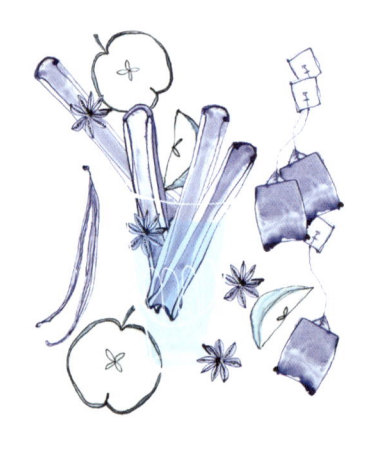

A Rockpool book
PO Box 252
Summer Hill
NSW 2130
Australia

rockpoolpublishing.co
Follow us! **f** 📷 rockpoolpublishing
Tag your images with #rockpoolpublishing

ISBN: 9781922579041

Published in 2022 by Rockpool Publishing
Copyright text and images © Tracy Loughlin, 2022
Copyright design © Rockpool Publishing, 2022

Design by Sara Lindberg, Rockpool Publishing

All rights reserved. No part of this publication may be reproduced, stored in a retrieval system, or transmitted in any form or by any means, electronic, mechanical, photocopying, recording or otherwise, without the prior written permission of the publisher.

Disclaimer: All teas are based on the personal experience of the author. The reader must take responsibility to test all ingredients to ensure they have no potential adverse effects. Adverse effects include allergies, issues arising due to health-related restricted diet and/or pregnancy-related effects. If any symptoms occur please seek medical advice.

Printed and bound in China
10 9 8 7 6 5 4 3 2 1

ROCKPOOL